The Book of the Watchers

Divine Mysteries of the Angels and the Origins of Humanity

A Modern Translation

Adapted for the Contemporary Reader

Enoch the Patriarch

Translated by Tim Zengerink

© **Copyright 2025**
All rights reserved.

It is not legal to reproduce, duplicate, or transmit any part of this document in either electronic means or in printed format. Recording of this publication is strictly prohibited and any storage of this document is not allowed unless with written permission from the publisher except for the use of brief quotations in a book review.

This book contains works of fiction. Any resemblance to persons living or dead, or places, events, or locations is purely coincidental.

Table Of Contents

Preface - Message to the Reader 1
Introduction 5
An Oracle of Judgment (1:2—5:9) 13
    PE Peophany 13
    PE Indictmenta 15
    PE Verdict 17
The Rebellion of The Watchers (Chapters 6–11) 18
    PE Conspiracy 18
    PE Deed and Its Results 19
    PE Secrets the Watchers Revealb 20
    PE Intercession of The Four Archangels 21
    PE Commissioning of The Four
        Archangels 23
Michael is to Renovate the Earth 25
Enoch's Interaction with The Fallen Watchers
Chapters 12–16) 27
    An Editorial Introduction 27
Enoch's First Mission to The Fallen Watchers 28
    PE Fallen Watchers Commission Enoch to
        Intercede for Pem 29
Enoch's Ascent to Heaven and Second
Commission to Preach to The Watchers 31

Narrative Summary 31
Enoch's Journey to The Northwest (Chapters 17–19) 37
  PE Journey Narrative Begun 37
A Digression: A Summary of What Enoch Saw 40
  PE Journey Narrative Concluded 42
Enoch's Journey Eastward (Chapters 20–36) 45
  List of The Seven Archangels 45
  PE Place of Punishment for The Disobedient Stars 47
  PE Prison of The Fallen Angels 48
  PE Mountain of The Dead 50
  PE Fire of The West 52
  PE Mountain Of God and The Tree of Life 52
Jerusalem, The Center of The Earth and The Place of Punishment 55
To The Paradise of Righteousness 57
To The Ends of The Earth 59
Enoch's Journeys North, West, South, And East 60
  A Summary 60
Thank You for Reading 62

Preface - Message to the Reader

What If You Could Help Rebuild the Greatest Library in Human History?

Thousands of years ago, the Library of Alexandria stood as the crown jewel of human achievement — a sanctuary where the collected wisdom of every known civilization was gathered, preserved, and shared freely.

And then, it was lost.

Through fire, conquest, and the slow erosion of time, humanity lost not just books — but ideas, dreams, discoveries, and stories that could have changed the world forever.

Today, the Library of Alexandria lives again — and you are invited to be a part of its restoration.

Our mission is simple yet profound:

To rebuild the greatest library the world has ever known, and to translate all timeless works into every language and dialect, so that no seeker of knowledge is ever left behind again.

By joining our movement to rebuild the modern Library of Alexandria, you become part of an unprecedented mission:

- **Unlimited Access to the Greatest Audiobooks & eBooks Ever Written:**

  Instantly explore thousands of legendary works—Plato, Shakespeare, Jane Austen, Leo Tolstoy, and countless more. All instantly available to read or listen, placing a complete literary universe at your fingertips.

- **Beautiful Paperback & Deluxe Editions at Printing Cost**

  Own any title as an elegant paperback, deluxe hardcover, or stunning collectible boxset—offered to you at true printing cost, delivered straight to your door. Build your personal Library of Alexandria, crafted for beauty, built for durability, and worthy of proud display.

- **Fresh Translations for Modern Readers—in Every Language & Dialect**

  Enjoy timeless masterpieces reimagined in clear, contemporary language—no more outdated phrases or obscure references. Alongside the original versions, we're tirelessly translating these classics into every language and dialect imaginable, ensuring accessibility and understanding across cultures and generations.

- **Join a Global Renaissance of Literature & Knowledge**

   You directly support expanding our library, publishing deluxe editions at true cost, translating works into all global languages, and bringing humanity's greatest stories to people everywhere. By joining today, you're not just preserving a legacy of masterpieces; you set in motion a powerful wave of literary accessibility.

Become a Torchbearer of Knowledge.

Join us for free now at **LibraryofAlexandria.com**

Together, we will ensure that the light of human wisdom never fades again.

With gratitude and a shared love of knowledge,

The Modern Library of Alexandria Team

Visit:

www.libraryofalexandria.com

Or scan the code below:

Introduction

The Descent of the Watchers and the Origins of Human Knowledge

The Book of the Watchers, the first and most widely read section of the larger work known as 1 Enoch, stands as one of the oldest and most influential texts in the apocalyptic tradition. Attributed to Enoch the Patriarch—seventh from Adam and a man said to have "walked with God"—this ancient narrative offers a sweeping and haunting vision of how divine order was disturbed, how humanity was shaped by contact with the celestial realm, and how divine judgment was prepared in response to an era of cosmic rebellion. More than a mythological tale or a mystical account, this is a theological exploration of justice, knowledge, corruption, and the structure of the spiritual universe. It is a story about angels who overstepped their boundaries, about forbidden wisdom that altered the course of history, and about a man chosen to witness, document, and ultimately intercede on behalf of all creation.

At the heart of the narrative is the descent of the Watchers, a group of angels originally tasked with observing and watching over humanity. In a fateful act of rebellion, these beings descend to Earth, captivated by human women and driven by desire to abandon their divine post. This transgression is not merely about lust; it is a violation of divine law and spiritual hierarchy. In taking wives for themselves and producing offspring—the Nephilim, giants of extraordinary power—they introduce a hybrid race that distorts the natural order. But the consequences go even further: the Watchers bring with them knowledge forbidden to humanity. They teach metallurgy, weapon-making, sorcery, astrology, cosmetics, and more—tools and insights that alter human life forever, some for advancement, many for destruction.

Through this act, The Book of the Watchers presents a unique vision of the origin of evil not as something created by God or innate to humanity, but as a result of celestial beings corrupting a fragile and unfinished creation. The narrative is not only concerned with physical consequences, such as violence and bloodshed, but with the moral and spiritual impact of this angelic defiance. Humanity, suddenly awakened to knowledge beyond its capacity to control, is thrown into a world of chaos, temptation, and judgment. In this framework, sin is not only a human failure—it is a cosmic event, one that disturbs the balance of heaven and earth.

Enoch, the central figure and narrator, is chosen by God to witness this drama and to mediate its consequences. He is taken on visionary journeys through the heavens, where he sees the structure of the cosmos, the prisons of the fallen angels, the throne of the Most High, and the scrolls of judgment. He receives knowledge from the angels, not to exploit, but to record and transmit with reverence and responsibility. In doing so, Enoch becomes the first great seer in biblical literature—a prophet of cosmic dimensions. His role is not only to reveal what he has seen but to intercede for both the angels and humanity, standing between worlds as a witness, messenger, and scribe of divine mysteries.

This work is more than a historical curiosity or a mystical fantasy. It is a profound meditation on the boundaries of knowledge, the ethics of power, and the purpose of divine revelation. The story of the Watchers is not merely about ancient angels and ancient humans—it is about the enduring questions that arise when knowledge is divorced from wisdom, when power is pursued without humility, and when divine gifts are used for selfish ends. These questions remain as urgent today as they were in the time of Enoch, making The Book of the Watchers not only a foundational apocalyptic text, but a timeless source of spiritual insight.

Translated by Tim Zengerink

Judgment, Cosmic Order, and the Role of Enoch

The second great theme of The Book of the Watchers is judgment. The transgressions of the Watchers and the violence unleashed by their offspring provoke a divine response. God, portrayed with grandeur and majesty, does not remain distant. He observes, weighs, and acts decisively to restore cosmic balance. The fallen angels are imprisoned in deep abysses, bound until the day of their final judgment. Their offspring, the Nephilim, are destroyed in a flood of divine wrath. But even more significant than the judgment itself is the process through which it is communicated and administered—through visions, angelic messengers, and ultimately through Enoch himself.

Enoch's role is essential. He does not simply report what he sees—he participates in the unfolding divine plan. He journeys through the heavens and records their structure. He visits the place of punishment and learns of its purpose. He hears the laments of the fallen angels and pleads their case, only to receive a clear and final verdict: their fate is sealed. This theme of intercession, denied and granted, weaves through the text and affirms Enoch's status as a spiritual mediator—one who speaks both to God and to humanity.

As he is drawn deeper into the divine mysteries, Enoch is shown the layout of creation, the courses of the stars and planets, the winds and the waters, and the foundations of the earth. This vision of cosmic order is central to the text's theology. Creation is not chaotic or random—it is structured, purposeful, and reflective of divine wisdom. The rebellion of the Watchers is tragic precisely because it defies this order. Knowledge, the text insists, is sacred. When misused or revealed prematurely, it becomes destructive. When preserved within the proper bounds of divine intention, it leads to wisdom, righteousness, and spiritual elevation.

The dual vision of punishment and order, destruction and stability, gives The Book of the Watchers its deep moral resonance. This is a text that refuses to separate cosmic revelation from ethical responsibility. It teaches that knowledge is a sacred trust, that sin has cosmic consequences, and that justice is not only retributive but restorative. The judgments rendered are severe, but they are part of a larger effort to purify the world, to restore its balance, and to reaffirm the authority of the Most High. In this way, the work is not merely a narrative of doom, but a message of hope. It affirms that God remains sovereign, that order will be restored, and that the righteous—those like Enoch—will be rewarded with eternal insight and peace.

This modern translation is designed to capture the depth and mystery of this extraordinary text while making it fully accessible to contemporary readers. Each sentence has been carefully adapted to preserve the structure and meaning of the original while presenting it in clear, fluid language. The archaic vocabulary and cryptic phrasing found in earlier translations have been revised without compromising the text's spiritual tone or theological weight. The result is a version that can be read not only with understanding but with reverence—one that invites reflection, study, and awe.

Engaging the Book Today: Timeless Themes and Enduring Power

Reading The Book of the Watchers today is an invitation into a spiritual and intellectual world that challenges many modern assumptions. It calls into question the uncritical pursuit of knowledge, the separation of the material from the spiritual, and the belief that humanity is the sole actor in the story of the universe. It suggests instead that there is a cosmic history behind human history, that our moral choices resonate beyond the visible world, and that divine judgment is not only real but necessary. It urges humility before mystery and warns against the arrogance that seeks to ascend without reverence.

At the same time, the story is profoundly hopeful. Enoch, the faithful scribe, stands as a symbol of what is possible when humanity aligns with divine wisdom. He listens rather than demands. He receives revelation not for pride, but for instruction. He becomes a bridge between heaven and earth—not through force, but through faithfulness. In a world that often values power over purity and achievement over integrity, Enoch's example is a quiet but resounding call to another way.

This modern adaptation seeks to preserve that call. It offers The Book of the Watchers not as a relic of a forgotten age, but as a living text—one that still speaks, still warns, still inspires. Whether you are reading it as a student of ancient religion, as a seeker of divine truth, or as someone simply drawn to the mystery of the unseen, you will find in these pages a wealth of insight. The questions it raises—about the limits of knowledge, the nature of rebellion, the structure of the cosmos, and the meaning of divine justice—are as vital today as they were thousands of years ago.

Let this text take you beyond the surface of the world into the depths of divine mystery. Let it open your eyes to the ancient belief that angels walk among us, that wisdom must be handled with care, and that every act ripples through the fabric of creation. Let it remind you, as it reminded its earliest readers, that there is more to the world than we can see—and that to truly understand our place within it, we must listen not only to what is visible, but to the voice of the One who made all things.

Enter The Book of the Watchers with reverence. Read it with attention. And emerge from it not only informed, but awakened.

An Oracle of Judgment (1:2—5:9)

And he started his message, saying:

"Enoch was a good man, and God helped him see clearly. He was shown a vision of the Holy One and heaven, and it was revealed to me as well. I heard everything from the watchers and the holy ones, and as I listened, I began to understand what I had seen.

This message is not for the people living now, but for those in a distant future.

Now, I will speak about those who have been chosen, because this message is meant for them."

PE Peophany

The Great Holy One will step out from His home,
and the eternal God will descend to stand on Mount Sinai.
He will come with His mighty army,
surrounded by countless powerful beings from heaven.

All the watchers will be filled with fear,
and those hiding in distant places will lift their voices in song.

Translated by Tim Zengerink

The whole earth will shake violently,
and terror will spread even to the farthest lands.

The highest mountains will tremble and break apart,
the tall hills will collapse and melt like wax in a fire.
The earth itself will be torn apart,
and everything on it will be destroyed, for judgment is coming to all.

But for those who do what is right, He will bring peace.
He will protect His chosen ones and surround them with mercy.
They will belong fully to Him, and He will take joy in them.
He will bless them, help them, and shine His light upon them.

Look, He is coming with countless holy ones,
to bring judgment upon the world,
to remove all who do evil,
and to hold everyone accountable for their wrong actions
and for the arrogant and cruel words that sinners have spoken against Him.

PE Indictmenta

Think about all of His works and the wonders of the sky. Notice how the heavens move exactly as they should, how the stars and lights in the sky rise and set at their proper times. Each one follows its path, marking the seasons and special days without ever changing from the order set for them.

Now, look at the earth and the amazing things that have happened on it since creation. Nothing truly changes because everything follows God's plan, steady and unshaken.

Pay attention to the seasons, the signs of summer and winter. Think about winter—how the ground becomes soaked with water, the sky fills with clouds, and rain and dew fall to nourish the land.

See how, in winter, most trees seem lifeless, their leaves dried up and gone. But there are fourteen trees that are different. They hold onto their old leaves until, after two or three years, new ones finally grow.

Now, think about the signs of summer. The sun shines with intense heat, burning the earth. You search for shade to escape its strength, while the ground becomes so hot that even the dust and stones seem to burn beneath your feet.

Translated by Tim Zengerink

Look at the trees in summer. Their leaves grow thick and green, covering the branches. Their fruit ripens in abundance, adding beauty and richness to the land.

When you see these wonders, remember that the One who lives forever created them all. Year after year, His works remain the same, each one serving its purpose just as He planned. Everything follows His command without fail.

Just as the sky and the earth obey Him, so do the seas and rivers. They continue their work without change, carrying out their tasks exactly as He directed.

But people have not remained faithful. They have turned away from His ways and ignored His commands. Instead, they have spoken with pride and arrogance, using their words to challenge His power.

You who are stubborn in your hearts—there will be no peace for you!

PE Verdict

Your life will be filled with regret, and the years you've lived will feel meaningless. The time of your downfall will turn into an endless curse, with no mercy or peace for you.

Your names will be remembered as a warning to others, and people will use them in their curses. The wicked will swear by your names, but those who are chosen will celebrate. They will receive forgiveness, kindness, and peace in abundance.

A bright light will shine on those who are chosen, and they will inherit the earth with happiness and peace. But for sinners, there will be no rescue—only a lasting curse.

The righteous will live in joy, surrounded by light and peace, while the wicked will face only misfortune.

Wisdom will be given to the chosen ones, and they will live without sin, free from arrogance and disbelief. They will gain understanding, and their minds will be filled with truth. They will no longer turn toward wrongdoing or disobey what is right.

They will not be destroyed by God's anger. Instead, they will live out their full days in peace, filled with joy, and they will remain in happiness forever.

The Rebellion of The Watchers (Chapters 6–11)

PE Conspiracy

As more people were born on the earth, many daughters grew up to be beautiful and attractive. The watchers, who were beings from the heavens, saw them and were overcome with desire. They said to each other, "Let's choose wives from among these women and have children with them."

Their leader, Shemihazah, warned them, "I'm afraid that you might change your minds, and I'll be the only one left to take the blame for this great sin."

But they all reassured him, saying, "Let's make a promise together and bind ourselves with a curse, so that no one backs out. We will go through with our plan no matter what."

So they swore an oath as a group and sealed it with a curse. There were two hundred of them in total, and they came down to earth during the time of Jared, landing on the top of Mount Hermon. They named the mountain "Hermon" because that was where they made their oath and bound themselves under the curse.

These were the names of their leaders: Shemihazah was their chief. Arteqoph was second, followed by Remashel, Kokabel, Armumahel, Ramel, Daniel, Ziqel, Baraqel, Asael, Hermani, Matarel, Anatel, Setawel, Samshiel, Sahriel, Tummiel, Turiel, Yamiel, and Yehadiel. These were the leaders of their groups.

PE Deed and Its Results

The watchers, along with those who followed them, chose wives from among human women, taking whoever they wanted. They lived with them, corrupting themselves through these relationships, and taught them things that were never meant to be known. They revealed the secrets of magic and spells and showed them how to use plants and roots for forbidden purposes.

The women became pregnant and gave birth to massive giants. These giants later had children of their own, called the Nephilim, and from the Nephilim came another generation known as the Elioud. Each new generation grew even larger and stronger.

The giants began taking everything that humans worked hard to produce, but no matter how much they took, it was never enough. When food ran out, they turned to violence, killing people to survive. Their evil only grew worse—they started harming birds, animals, and even fish, eating their flesh and drinking their blood.

The earth itself could no longer endure their cruelty, and it cried out against them.

Secrets the Watchers Reveal

Asael taught people how to make weapons, showing them how to forge swords from iron and craft shields, armor, and other tools for battle. He also introduced them to the metals found in the earth, teaching them how to shape gold into jewelry and silver into bracelets and decorations for women. He even showed them how to use antimony for makeup, craft beautiful stones, and create colorful dyes.

People eagerly used this knowledge, making weapons and ornaments for themselves and their daughters. But with this new knowledge, they strayed from the right path, leading others away from what was holy. Wickedness spread quickly, and humanity became more corrupt.

Shemihazah taught the secrets of spells and how to use plants for magic. Hermani revealed sorcery, ways to break spells, and other magical practices. Baraqel explained how to interpret lightning, while Kokabel taught about the stars. Ziqel showed the meaning of shooting stars, Arteqoph revealed signs from the earth, Shamsiel taught the movement of the sun, and Sahriel explained the phases of the moon.

These watchers shared their forbidden knowledge with their wives and children, revealing mysteries that were never meant to be known. As humanity became more corrupt, suffering and death increased. The cries of those in pain reached up to the heavens.

PE Intercession of The Four Archangels

Michael, Sariel, Raphael, and Gabriel looked down from the heights of heaven and saw the earth covered in violence and bloodshed. Wickedness had spread everywhere, corrupting the land.

They turned to one another and said, "The earth is filled with suffering, and the cries of the innocent rise up to heaven. The souls of those who have been wronged call out to us, pleading, 'Take our case before the Most High. Bring justice for our destruction before the Lord, the ruler of all.'"

They approached the presence of the Eternal Lord and said, "You are the God above all, the King of kings, the everlasting ruler of every age. Your throne stands firm from the beginning of time and will last forever. Your name is holy, great, and blessed for all eternity.

"You created everything, and your power rules over

all that exists. Nothing is hidden from you—every action, every secret is laid bare before your eyes. You see all things, and nothing escapes your knowledge.

"You have seen what Asael has done. He has revealed forbidden secrets to humanity—mysteries that were meant to stay hidden in heaven. Because of him, people have fallen deeper into sin, chasing after knowledge they were never meant to have.

"Shemihazah, whom you placed in charge of his followers, has also disobeyed you. He and his companions have taken human women for themselves, lying with them and corrupting them with sin. They have taught them sorcery and charms that spread hatred and destruction.

"The women have given birth to their children—giants, born from both heaven and earth. These creatures have filled the world with violence, spilling innocent blood and spreading wickedness across the land.

"The souls of those who have died cry out to you without rest. Their voices rise to heaven, pleading for justice against the sins that have overtaken the earth.

"Lord, you know all things before they even happen. You have seen all of this unfold, yet you have not told us what must be done. How should we bring justice for the wrongs that have been committed?"

PE Commissioning of The Four Archangels

The Most High spoke, and the Great Holy One made His decision known. He sent Sariel to deliver a message to Noah, the son of Lamech.

"Go to Noah and tell him in My name, 'Take shelter.' Warn him that the end is near, and the whole earth will be destroyed. A great flood is coming—a massive storm that will sweep across the land and wipe out all life. Teach this righteous man, the son of Lamech, what he must do to survive and escape this disaster. From him, a new generation will rise, one that will last for all time."

Then the Lord gave Raphael a command: "Raphael, go and capture Asael. Tie his hands and feet, and throw him into the darkness. Make an opening in the desert at Doudael, cast him inside, and place sharp, jagged stones beneath him. Cover him in darkness, so he will never see the light again. He will remain there for a long time, until the great day of judgment, when he will be thrown into the fire.

Heal the earth, which has been ruined by the Watchers, and restore it so that humanity does not perish because of the forbidden knowledge they passed down. The world was left in chaos because of Asael's teachings, and his sins must be recorded against him."

The Lord then turned to Gabriel and said, "Gabriel, go and deal with the children born from these forbidden unions—the hybrids, the offspring of the Watchers. Let them turn against each other and destroy themselves in a great war. They will not live long lives, and their fathers' pleas will not be heard. They will have no hope for eternal life, and none of them will live beyond five hundred years."

Finally, He spoke to Michael: "Michael, capture Shemihazah and all those who took human women as their own and corrupted themselves with them. When their sons have been destroyed and they have seen the loss of their loved ones, bind these Watchers and imprison them in the depths of the earth for seventy generations. They will remain there until the day of their judgment and final punishment.

On that day, they will be thrown into the fire, where they will suffer forever. All those who are condemned will be bound together with them until their time is finished. When judgment comes, they will be erased from existence for all eternity. Destroy the spirits of the hybrids and the sons of the Watchers, for they have brought suffering to humanity and ruin to the earth."

Michael is to Renovate the Earth

Remove every trace of evil from the earth, wiping out all acts of wrongdoing completely. Let goodness and truth grow strong, like a thriving plant, bringing blessings to everyone. Righteousness and honesty will take root forever, filling the world with joy and peace.

During this time, all who live righteously will be safe. They will enjoy long, full lives, growing in number, and both the young and old will live in peace, without fear or trouble.

The whole earth will be transformed into a paradise, filled with trees and overflowing with blessings. Every joyful tree will be planted, and vineyards will cover the land. Each vine will produce a thousand jugs of wine, and every seed planted will bring an incredible harvest. Olive trees will be abundant, producing more oil than ever before.

The world will be cleansed of every impurity, injustice, and sin. All corruption and wrongdoing that once polluted the earth will be completely wiped away.

Then, humanity itself will be changed. People will choose to live righteously, and all nations will worship and honor their Creator. They will praise His name and show Him respect and devotion.

The earth will be purified, free from anything unclean or corrupt. Never again will disaster or punishment come upon its people for all future generations.

At that time, the heavens will open and pour out blessings upon the world, enriching the work of human hands.

Truth and peace will stand together, side by side, lasting forever. These gifts will remain for all generations, bringing eternal harmony and prosperity to humankind.

Enoch's Interaction with The Fallen Watchers Chapters 12–16)

An Editorial Introduction

Before all these things happened, Enoch disappeared, and no one knew where he had gone or what had happened to him. His life was deeply connected to the watchers, and he spent his days among the holy ones.

Enoch's First Mission to The Fallen Watchers

Enoch Is Sent to the Watchers

I, Enoch, stood in awe, praising the Lord of majesty, the eternal King. Suddenly, the watchers of the Great Holy One called out to me, addressing me as Enoch the scribe. They said,

"Enoch, righteous scribe, go and deliver a message to the watchers of heaven—those who abandoned their sacred home and corrupted themselves by being with human women. Like the men of earth, they took wives for themselves, bringing great destruction upon the world.

Tell them, 'You will have no peace and no forgiveness. As for your children, whom you cherish—

you will see them destroyed.

You will mourn their loss,

and though you beg for mercy, none will be given to you.'

Enoch, also take this message to Asael: 'There will be no peace for you. A harsh judgment has been decided against you, and you will be bound. No relief or forgiveness will come for the evil you revealed—the corruption, sin, and lawlessness you taught to humanity.'"

Then I went and delivered this message to all of them together. When they heard it, they were overcome with fear, trembling as terror filled them.

PE Fallen Watchers Commission Enoch to Intercede for Pem

They begged me to write a request on their behalf, a petition that might bring them forgiveness. They wanted me to bring it before the Lord of heaven. They were so ashamed of what they had done and the punishment they faced that they couldn't even look up toward heaven or speak for themselves.

I wrote down their plea, listing each of their requests, along with the details of their actions. They also asked for mercy for their children, hoping they would be allowed to live longer. After finishing the petition, I traveled to the waters of Dan, in the land of Dan, west of Mount Hermon. There, I sat down and read their plea aloud to God.

Translated by Tim Zengerink

As I prayed for them, the weight of their words and my responsibility became too much, and I eventually fell asleep.

Enoch's Ascent to Heaven and Second Commission to Preach to The Watchers

Narrative Summary

As I rested, vivid dreams filled my mind, and visions overwhelmed me like a rushing flood. I saw images of judgment and wrath, and in the midst of them, a powerful voice commanded, "Go to the watchers and deliver a message of warning." When I woke up, I immediately set out to find them.

I came upon the watchers, gathered in sorrow at Abel Main, a place between Lebanon and Senir. They sat together, weeping bitterly, their faces covered in shame. Standing before them, I recounted every vision I had seen in my dream. I spoke the words of truth and the warning I had been given to deliver.

This is the record, written as The Book of the Words of Truth and the Warning to the Watchers Who Have Been Here Since Ancient Times, as commanded by the Great Holy One in my dream. I share what I saw with my human voice, using the breath the Creator has given mankind for speech and understanding. Just as

He created people to comprehend wisdom, He chose me to deliver this message to the watchers, the sons of heaven.

I wrote down your petition as you requested, but in the vision, it was made clear—your request will not be granted. Not now, not ever. Judgment has been made, and you will never return to heaven again. You will remain bound to the earth forever.

But before this happens, you will witness the destruction of your children, those you love most. You will watch as they are killed, and their deaths will bring you no comfort. You will beg for mercy, but none will come. No part of the petition I wrote will be fulfilled.

In the vision, I saw more: clouds gathered, calling out to me, and mist rose up, summoning me. Shooting stars and flashes of lightning pulled me forward, carrying me upward. Powerful winds lifted me from all directions, raising me into the heavens.

I arrived at a massive wall, shining like ice, surrounded by tongues of fire that flickered and danced. Fear gripped me, but I pressed on and stepped into the flames.

Inside, I saw an enormous and magnificent house, made entirely of glistening ice. The walls were bright and white like snow, and the floor beneath me was pure ice. Above, the ceiling sparkled with the brilliance of shooting stars and flashes of lightning. Fiery beings moved through the space, and the sky itself looked like flowing water. A ring of fire surrounded the entire structure, and the doors burned with an unquenchable flame.

I entered, but the place was filled with extremes—burning heat like fire and freezing cold like ice. It was unlike anything I had ever known, lifeless and overwhelming. Fear took hold of me, and I began to tremble. My strength left me, and I collapsed, my face to the ground.

Then I saw something even greater: another house, far more magnificent than the first. It was built entirely of fire, radiating a brilliance beyond words. The entire floor burned with flames, and the upper portion flashed with lightning and shooting stars. Even the ceiling was covered in fire, filling the space with an overwhelming presence.

As I looked further, I saw a towering throne. It shined like crystal, and its wheels blazed as bright as the sun. Around it, countless fiery beings sang in harmony. Beneath the throne, rivers of fire flowed endlessly. The sight was beyond my understanding.

Seated on the throne was a figure whose presence lit up everything. His clothing shone like the sun, brighter than the purest snow, and His radiance was unmatched. No angel dared to enter or even look at Him because His brilliance was too overwhelming. No human could withstand His glory. Flames surrounded Him, and a great fire stood beside Him. None of those around Him dared to approach.

Before Him stood countless multitudes—ten thousand times ten thousand—but He needed no advisor, for His very words brought things into existence.

The holy ones closest to Him remained in His presence at all times, never leaving, always devoted to His glory.

As I lay trembling before Him, the Lord suddenly called my name: "Come here, Enoch, and listen to My words."

One of the holy ones came forward, lifted me up, and helped me stand, but I kept my face lowered, unable to look at the One before me.

Then the voice of the Great One spoke again, calming my fear: "Do not be afraid, Enoch, righteous man and scribe of truth. Come closer and hear what I have to say. Go and speak to the watchers who sent you to plead for them. Tell them this:

'It is not for humans to intercede for you; you were meant to intercede for them. Why did you leave the heights of heaven, your eternal home, and defile yourselves with human women? You became like mortal men, taking wives and fathering children—giants born from your union. You were created as spirits, meant to live forever, but you corrupted yourselves with lust, a desire meant only for those who die.

I gave men wives so they could continue their lineage and sustain life on earth. But you—your existence was never meant to rely on such things. Your home was in heaven, not on earth, and I did not create wives for you.

Now, the spirits of the giants—born from the union of heavenly beings and humans—have become evil spirits on the earth. Though they came from human mothers, they are corrupted by the watchers who fathered them. They will remain on earth as wicked spirits, leading people astray.

These spirits will cause violence, destruction, and suffering. They will spread sickness, attack humanity, and bring harm to women. Though they do not eat, they are always hungry, and though they do not drink, they remain thirsty, causing endless misery.

Since the day the giants were killed, their spirits have wandered the earth, bringing destruction without being judged. This will continue until the final day of judgment when all things will be set right.

Now, go and tell the watchers who sent you to plead for them: You once lived in heaven, but you betrayed your place. No secrets were ever entrusted to you, yet you stole forbidden knowledge and taught it to women. Because of this, human wickedness has multiplied, and corruption has spread across the earth.

Tell them plainly: 'You will find no peace.'"

Enoch's Journey to The Northwest (Chapters 17–19)

PE Journey Narrative Begun

They took me to a place unlike anything I had ever seen. The beings who lived there were made of fire, their bodies glowing and burning with an intense energy. Yet, when they wanted to, they could take on human form, hiding their fiery nature. Watching them change left me in awe, for their transformations were beyond anything I could understand.

From there, they led me into deep darkness. Before me stood an enormous mountain, so tall its peak seemed to touch the heavens. Standing at its base, I could feel its power and the mysteries it held. They guided me further, and I saw the realm of the stars and celestial lights. Here were the places where their brightness was stored, along with the chambers of thunder, where powerful roars echoed. The very fabric of the sky was revealed to me, showing bows of fire, flaming arrows, quivers filled with burning shafts, and even a sword made entirely of fire. Flashes of lightning surrounded me, lighting up the darkness with their dazzling brilliance.

Next, they took me to the source of living waters—streams flowing with life and mystery. From there, I was led to a great fire in the west, the force behind the setting sun, painting the sky with its warm, glowing colors every evening. This fire had an everlasting power, its presence felt in the fading light of every day.

Then, I came to a river unlike any other—a river of fire, flowing as freely as water. Its blazing currents rushed downward into a massive sea in the west, where the fiery stream merged with the dark waters, casting a shimmering glow across its surface. It was both breathtaking and terrifying, a reminder of forces far beyond human control.

As my journey continued, I was shown all the great rivers of the earth, their waters winding through the land. Eventually, I reached a powerful river that led into a vast darkness. There was no light, and as I moved forward, I entered a place untouched by human feet. The land was silent, untouched, filled with an eerie stillness.

Here, I saw the cold, howling winds of darkness, relentless and unyielding as they swept through the void. Deep waters gushed from hidden depths, their sources unknown and impossible to understand. I stood before the mouths of all the rivers of the world, each one pouring its waters into this unseen realm. Finally, I arrived at the edge of the abyss itself—a vast, endless chasm, so deep and consuming that it felt like it held the very secrets of creation.

A Digression:
A Summary of What Enoch Saw

I was shown the great storehouses of the winds, vast and complex places where the forces that move the air across the sky and the earth are kept. Through these winds, the Creator brings balance to everything, placing each part of creation exactly where it belongs. Though invisible, their power shapes the natural world, connecting the sky and the land in ways beyond human understanding.

My vision reached the very foundation of the earth, where I saw its mighty cornerstone. It was a structure of unshakable strength, holding all of creation in place. I saw the four great winds that support both the earth and the heavens above. Though unseen, these winds serve as the pillars of the sky, keeping everything in perfect balance.

I watched as the winds stretched high, lifting the heavens and holding them in place. They formed an invisible link between the earth and the sky, creating a bridge that supports the heavens. These winds are the framework upon which the vast sky rests, ensuring harmony between the realms above and below.

I saw how the winds of heaven guided the movements of the celestial bodies. They turned the great circle of the sun, directing it toward its setting with perfect accuracy, and they led the stars on their paths across the night sky. These winds did not move randomly, but followed a set order, their motions controlled by divine wisdom.

Then I looked toward the earth and saw the winds carrying the clouds. Sometimes they moved them gently, while at other times they pushed them forward with great force, spreading rain and shade across the land. I also saw the paths of the angels, moving between the sky and the earth as they carried out their duties. These paths shone brightly and were perfectly ordered, a reflection of their divine purpose.

At last, I reached the farthest edge of the earth, where the sky above formed a great boundary between the land and the heavens. Here, the connection between the earthly and the celestial became clear. It was a breathtaking sight, revealing the beauty of creation and the careful way the heavens and the earth were woven together. I stood in awe, amazed at the infinite power and wisdom of the Creator.

Translated by Tim Zengerink

PE Journey Narrative Concluded

I arrived at a place where fire burned without end, day and night. In the midst of this blazing land stood seven enormous mountains made of precious stones, more magnificent than anything I had ever seen. Three were to the east and three to the south, each glowing with an otherworldly beauty.

The eastern mountains shimmered with colors of rare gems—pearl, jasper, and dazzling stones that seemed to shine with life. The mountains to the south glowed with fiery red stones, their surfaces flickering like flames. The tallest mountain among them stretched high into the sky, its peak like a grand throne made of antimony, crowned with a brilliant blue top of lapis lazuli. The entire scene was surrounded by flames that never faded, burning with an intense and sacred fire.

Beyond these mountains, I reached what seemed to be the very edge of the world. Here, the sky met its boundary, and the vast universe appeared to come to an end. A deep chasm lay before me, surrounded by towering pillars of fire. These fiery columns stretched endlessly in both directions—soaring into the sky and plunging into the depths below, lighting up the darkness of the abyss.

Standing beside me, Uriel explained the meaning of this place. "Here," he said, "are the angels who broke the laws of heaven. They took human women as their own and fathered children. Their spirits have changed form many times, bringing destruction to humanity and leading people to worship false gods. They will continue to mislead mankind until the day of final judgment, when they will receive their punishment. Their wives will also suffer for their sins, becoming sirens, forever trapped by their wrongdoing."

Moving past the chasm, I entered a place that felt completely abandoned. There was no sky above and no solid ground below. No water flowed, and no birds flew there. It was an empty void, terrifying in its silence and lifelessness.

In this desolate space, I saw seven stars, burning like massive mountains of fire. I asked the angel with me what they were, and he explained:

"This is the outermost edge of heaven and earth. It is the prison where rebellious stars and heavenly beings are kept. These stars once had a purpose, but they defied the Creator's command. They failed to appear at their appointed times, and because of their disobedience, the Lord has bound them here in fire. They will remain imprisoned until the time of judgment, when their sins will finally be accounted for—ten thousand years from now."

Beyond all these visions, I, Enoch, saw the farthest reaches of creation. No other human has witnessed what I have seen—the ends of the heavens and the earth, the hidden truths of the stars, and the fate of those who fell from grace. These revelations were shown to me alone, revealing the deep and mysterious forces that shape existence.

Enoch's Journey Eastward (Chapters 20–36)

List of The Seven Archangels

These are the names of the seven holy angels, each given a special duty by the Creator. They watch over the world and carry out God's will with wisdom and care.

Uriel is one of the sacred angels. He is responsible for watching over the world and Tartarus, the deep abyss where rebellious spirits are sent. He ensures that divine justice is carried out, keeping order in both the earth and the underworld.

Raphael is in charge of human souls. He protects and guides them, making sure they follow the path meant for them. He is also known as a healer and guardian, bringing comfort and protection to people.

Reuel is responsible for enforcing justice among the celestial bodies. He ensures that the stars and heavenly lights follow their intended course and that no power is misused.

Michael is the great archangel assigned to protect the righteous. He stands as a leader and defender of those who are faithful, guiding them in their struggles against evil. He is a strong and powerful protector of God's people.

Sariel is given authority over spirits that sin against the spirit. He deals with those who go beyond ordinary wrongdoing, committing offenses that disrupt the divine order. He ensures that they face the consequences of their actions.

Gabriel is the guardian of paradise. He watches over the garden of eternal life, as well as the serpents and cherubim that dwell there. His duty is to keep paradise pure and untouched, making sure it remains a place of divine beauty.

Remiel is the angel responsible for those who rise again. He oversees resurrection, guiding souls as they ascend to their destined place in the divine order.

These seven angels—Uriel, Raphael, Reuel, Michael, Sariel, Gabriel, and Remiel—are the great archangels of the Lord. Each carries out their mission with absolute devotion, ensuring the balance of creation and carrying out God's justice in both heaven and earth. Their names reflect their sacred roles and the divine order established by God.

PE Place of Punishment for The Disobedient Stars

I traveled to a place filled with disorder and confusion, unlike anything I had ever seen. There was no sky above to bring light or hope, and no solid ground beneath to provide stability. Everything around me felt unstable, as if nothing had a true form or foundation. It was a space of chaos, overwhelming and unsettling.

In the middle of this place, I saw something that filled me with both awe and fear—seven stars, chained together and trapped in this stormy void. They were massive, like towering mountains, and covered in flames that burned endlessly, consuming them without rest.

Shaken by what I saw, I turned and asked, "Why are these stars bound like this? What did they do to deserve such a punishment?"

Uriel, one of the holy angels who was guiding me, stood nearby. He looked at me and replied, "Enoch, why do you seek to understand this? Why do you want to know the reason behind what you see?"

Then he explained their fate to me. "These stars are not just celestial bodies; they were once part of the heavens. But they disobeyed the commands of the Lord, refusing to follow the paths set for them. Because of their rebellion, they have been locked away in this fiery prison. They will remain here for ten thousand years—until the time of their judgment has been fulfilled."

His words weighed heavily on me. I stood in silence, trying to grasp the meaning of what I had witnessed. Around us, the chaos of this place raged like a storm without end.

PE Prison of The Fallen Angels

From there, I was taken to an even more terrifying place than the one before. As I got closer, a deep sense of fear and unease filled me. What I saw was beyond anything I had ever imagined. A massive fire raged, its flames roaring and leaping as if they were alive. This was not an ordinary fire—it moved with power and fury, burning endlessly with an intensity that seemed unnatural.

In this dreadful place, I saw a deep, narrow chasm stretching far into the abyss. Around it stood enormous pillars of fire, each one plunging into the darkness below. The sight was both fascinating and horrifying, as the depth of the abyss and the size of the fiery pillars seemed impossible to measure or fully understand. No matter how hard I tried, I couldn't grasp how vast it truly was—it seemed to stretch on forever, disappearing into the shadows.

Overwhelmed by the horror of what I was witnessing, I cried out, "This place is beyond terrifying! No one should ever have to see something so dreadful!"

At that moment, Uriel, one of the holy angels guiding me, stepped forward. His presence was calm, completely different from the chaos and fear surrounding us. He turned to me and asked, "Enoch, why are you so afraid? Why does this sight shake you so much?"

Still trembling, I answered, "How could I not be? This place is beyond anything I can bear. Just looking at it fills me with fear, and everything about it is horrifying."

Uriel then spoke again, his voice steady and full of authority. "This place is a prison. It is where the rebellious angels have been locked away, and here they will remain forever. Their punishment will never end, and this fiery abyss will be their eternal home."

As I took in his words, I felt the weight of their meaning pressing down on me. This was not just a place of fire and destruction—it was a warning, a symbol of divine justice. The flames and the endless abyss stood as a reminder of the price of disobedience, their presence forever marking the consequences of defying the will of the Almighty.

Translated by Tim Zengerink

PE Mountain of The Dead

From there, I was taken to another place, where I saw a huge mountain of solid rock in the west. Inside the mountain were four deep and smooth hollow spaces. Three of them were dark, while one was bright and filled with light. In the center of the bright hollow, a fountain of water flowed.

I looked at the hollows and said, "These spaces are so deep and smooth, but why do they look so dark?"

Then Raphael, one of the holy angels with me, answered, "These hollows were created to hold the spirits of the dead. This is their purpose. Every soul comes here after death. These are the places where they are kept, waiting until the final day of judgment."

As I stood there, I heard the spirit of a man crying out, his voice filled with pain and desperation. His sorrowful cries rose up toward heaven as he pleaded for justice.

I turned to Raphael and asked, "Who is this spirit crying out so desperately?"

Raphael replied, "This is the spirit of Abel, who was killed by his brother Cain. Abel's spirit calls out against Cain and will continue to do so until all of Cain's descendants are wiped from the earth."

Then I asked about the different hollow spaces, wanting to understand why they were separated.

Raphael explained, "Each hollow was made for a different group of spirits.

The first hollow, the bright one with the fountain, is for the spirits of the righteous. This is where those who lived good and faithful lives are gathered.

The second hollow is for sinners—those who died without being judged for their wrongdoing while they were alive. Their spirits suffer in this place, waiting for the great day of judgment when they will receive their final punishment. They will remain bound here forever.

The third hollow is for the spirits of those who were murdered. These spirits cry out for justice, revealing the pain and destruction they suffered at the hands of evildoers.

The fourth hollow is for the spirits of the godless—those who lived in sin and walked alongside the wicked. These spirits will never rise again, and they will never receive a second chance at life."

Hearing this, I praised the Lord and said, "Righteous is Your judgment! Blessed are You, Lord of majesty and justice, the eternal ruler of all time!"

Translated by Tim Zengerink

PE Fire of The West

From there, I traveled to another place, far to the west at the edge of the earth. I saw a fire that never went out—it burned endlessly, moving day and night without ever stopping.

I asked, "What is this fire that never stops?"

Reuel, one of the holy angels with me, answered, "This is the fire of the west. It follows the paths of the heavenly lights as they move through the sky."

Then he showed me mountains made of fire, burning without end, their flames glowing both day and night.

PE Mountain Of God and The Tree of Life

I continued my journey and came upon seven magnificent mountains, each unique and dazzling with precious stones. Their beauty was breathtaking, and they shone brightly in the light. Three of them stood to the east, stacked one above the other, and three to the south, also layered the same way. Between them were deep, rugged valleys that never met.

The seventh mountain stood in the center, taller than all the others. It had the shape of a throne, and around it grew many fragrant trees. Among them was one unlike any I had ever seen. Its scent was sweeter than any spice, and its leaves, blossoms, and branches never withered. The fruit it bore looked like dates from palm trees and seemed perfect in every way.

I said, "This tree is incredible! Its fragrance is amazing, its leaves are beautiful, and its blossoms are stunning."

Then Michael, one of the holy angels with me and their leader, spoke and said, "Enoch, why are you so curious about this tree? Why do you wonder about its fragrance and beauty? Do you wish to understand its purpose?"

I replied, "Yes, I want to know everything, but especially about this tree."

Michael answered, "The tall mountain you see, the one shaped like a throne, is where the Great Holy One, the Lord of Glory, the King of Eternity, will sit when He comes to visit the earth with goodness.

As for this special tree, no human may touch it until the great day of judgment, when justice is served, and everything is brought to completion. After that, it will be given to the righteous and the faithful. They will eat its fruit, and it will be placed near God's holy dwelling, beside the house of the Eternal King.

Then the righteous will rejoice, full of happiness as they enter the holy sanctuary. The tree's fragrance will fill their very bones, and they will live long, joyful lives, just as their ancestors did in the past. They will no longer suffer pain, hardship, or disease."

Hearing this, I praised the God of Glory, the Eternal King, who has prepared such wonderful blessings for the righteous and has promised to share them with His people.

Jerusalem, The Center of The Earth and The Place of Punishment

From there, I traveled to the center of the earth, where I saw a beautiful and blessed land. It was filled with trees that stayed green and kept growing without end. In this place, there was also a holy mountain.

From beneath the mountain, a stream of water flowed eastward and continued south. To the east of this mountain, I saw another mountain, even taller, and between the two was a deep, narrow valley with water running beneath the mountain.

To the west of the first mountain, I saw a smaller mountain, not very tall. Below it was a deep, dry valley. Another deep and dry valley lay at the point where the three mountains met. These valleys were carved from solid rock, with no trees or life growing in them.

I was amazed by the sight of the mountains and the valleys, unable to comprehend what I was seeing.

I asked, "Why is this land so blessed, filled with trees, while this valley is barren and lifeless?"

Sariel, one of the holy angels with me, answered,

"This valley is cursed. It is meant for those who are condemned forever. It is the place where those who have spoken against the Lord and dishonored His name will be gathered. They will remain here until the final days, when they will face judgment in the presence of the righteous for all eternity. Even in this place, the godless will recognize the Lord's greatness and bless His name.

During their judgment, they will finally understand His mercy and the kindness they were given."

Hearing this, I praised the Lord of glory, declaring His greatness and honoring Him with deep respect.

To The Paradise of Righteousness

I traveled to a mountain range in the middle of the desert. Most of the land was dry and barren, except for one area filled with trees and plants. A large stream of water flowed down from above, spreading like a wide river toward the northwest, carrying water and moisture to the land.

From there, I moved east of the mountains and came to another part of the desert. In the fields, I saw trees that smelled like frankincense and myrrh, and they looked similar to nut trees.

Continuing farther east, I reached a vast land filled with valleys of water. In these valleys, I saw fragrant plants growing, similar to reeds. Along the banks, the air was filled with the sweet scent of cinnamon.

Beyond these valleys, I traveled even farther east and came to another mountain range. The mountains were covered with trees that produced a fragrant nectar called storax and galbanum. Beyond these mountains, I found another covered in aloe trees. These trees were full of sap, and their bark looked like that of almond trees. When ground into powder, the bark released a fragrance sweeter than any perfume.

Continuing to the northeast, I saw more mountains filled with the finest spices—nard, tspr, cardamom, and pepper. From there, I journeyed even farther east, reaching the farthest parts of the earth. I crossed the Red Sea and traveled far beyond it. As I continued, I passed through a region of complete darkness and kept moving forward.

Eventually, I came near the paradise of righteousness. From a distance, I saw trees larger and more numerous than any I had seen before. These trees were different—massive, beautiful, and majestic. Among them stood a special tree, the tree of wisdom. Its fruit was eaten by the holy ones to gain great knowledge. The tree was as tall as a fir tree, with leaves similar to those of a carob tree. Its fruit grew in clusters like grapes, spreading a pleasant fragrance far and wide.

I said, "This tree is so beautiful! It looks so pleasing."

Then Gabriel, the holy angel with me, said, "This is the tree of wisdom. Long ago, your first father and mother ate from it. When they did, they gained knowledge, their eyes were opened, and they realized they were naked. Because of this, they were sent out of the garden."

To The Ends of The Earth

I continued my journey to the farthest edges of the earth, where I saw enormous creatures, each one different from the others. I also saw many kinds of birds, each with its own unique shape, beauty, and voice. No two were alike.

To the east of these creatures, I reached the very edge of the earth, where the sky touches the land and the gates of heaven open. I watched as the stars appeared, coming forth through these gates. I counted each one and carefully recorded their numbers, names, positions, movements, and the times and months when they appeared, just as Uriel, the holy angel guiding me, had taught me.

He explained everything in detail, writing down their names, the times they were meant to shine, and the purpose they were created to fulfill.

Enoch's Journeys
North, West, South, And East

A Summary

I continued my journey to the north, reaching the farthest edges of the earth, where I saw incredible and amazing sights. At the very edge, I saw three gates in the sky, standing open. From these gates, the northern winds blew out. Some winds brought cold air, hail, frost, snow, dew, and rain. One of the gates released winds that were gentle and beneficial, but the other two sent out powerful winds that caused storms and hardship on the earth.

From there, I traveled west, to the farthest part of the earth, where I saw three more heavenly gates, just like the ones in the east. They had the same number of openings and let out the same kinds of winds.

Then I journeyed south, to the ends of the earth, where I saw three more heavenly gates. From these gates, the southern winds blew, carrying dew and rain.

Finally, I traveled east, reaching the farthest part of the world. There, I saw three more heavenly gates, but above them were smaller openings. Through these smaller gates, the stars of heaven passed as they moved westward, following their set paths in the sky.

After witnessing all these things, I praised—and will always praise—the Lord of glory, who created such wonderful and powerful works. He has shown His mighty deeds to His angels and to the spirits of humanity, so they may recognize His power, honor His creation, and bless Him forever.

Thank You for Reading

Dear Reader,

We hope this timeless classic has sparked your imagination and enriched your literary journey. Now that you've turned the final page, we want to share a vision for the future of reading—one where every classic you've ever wanted to explore is at your fingertips, in a format that best suits your life.

We'd like to invite you to gain immediate, unlimited digital & audiobook access to hundreds of the most treasured literary classics ever written—along with the option to secure deluxe paperback, hardcover & box set editions at printing cost. Together, we can spark a new global literary renaissance alongside our small, independent publishing house called "The Library of Alexandria."

Thousands of years ago, the Library of Alexandria stood as a beacon of knowledge—until it was lost to history. We aim to reignite that spirit of preservation and discovery right now, in the modern age—only this time, it's accessible to all, in every language and every format.

Picture a world where every timeless classic, novel, poem, or philosophical treatise is not only available to read but also updated for today's readers—modernized, translated into any language or dialect, and ready to enjoy in any format you choose, whether that is in an eBook, audiobook, paperback, or deluxe hardcover & box set version a printing cost.

By joining our movement to rebuild the modern Library of Alexandria, you become part of an unprecedented mission to offer:

- **Unlimited Audiobook & eBook Access to the Greatest Classics of All Time**

    Instantly explore thousands of legendary works, from Plato and Shakespeare to Jane Austen and Leo Tolstoy. All are instantly ready to read or listen to, giving you a complete literary universe at your fingertips.

- **Paperback & Deluxe Editions at Printing Costs:**

    Purchase any title in a paperback, deluxe hardbound, or deluxe boxset edition at printing costs, shipped right to your doorstep. Curate your personal library of Alexandria with editions worthy of display— crafted to last, designed to captivate, and delivered straight to your door.

- **Modern translations for Contemporary Readers in all languages and dialects**

    Discover a vast selection of classics reimagined in clear, current language—no more struggling with outdated phrases or obscure references. Next to the original versions, we aim to offer translations in as many languages and dialects as possible.

    As we continue our translation efforts and add new languages, readers everywhere can connect with these works as if they were written today. By bridging linguistic divides, you're contributing to ensuring that these timeless stories become more meaningful, accessible, and inspiring for people across the globe.

- **Your Personal Library of Alexandria:**

    Over the months and years, you'll curate a unique physical archive of classics—each volume a testament to your taste, curiosity, and love of knowledge. It's not just about owning books—it's about curating a cultural legacy you'll cherish and pass down for generations to come.

- **Join a Global Literary Renaissance:**

    Your support fuels an ongoing mission: allowing us to reinvest in offering deluxe print editions (including special boxsets) at their true cost, broaden the range of available formats and translations, and extend the reach of these works to new audiences worldwide. By joining today, you're not just preserving a legacy of masterpieces; you set in motion a powerful wave of literary accessibility.

We are more than a publisher—we're a movement, and we can't do it alone. Your support lets us scale our mission, preserving and reimagining history's greatest works for tomorrow's readers.

Become a Torchbearer of knowledge.

Thank you for picking up this book and allowing us into your literary journey. As you turn the pages, know that you're part of something larger: a global effort to keep these stories alive, share their wisdom across borders and generations, and spark a true cultural revival for the modern era.

If this resonates with you—please consider taking the next step by visiting:

www.libraryofalexandria.com

With gratitude and a shared love of knowledge,

The Modern Library of Alexandria Team

Visit:

www.libraryofalexandria.com

Or scan the code below:

www.ingramcontent.com/pod-product-compliance
Lightning Source LLC
LaVergne TN
LVHW030631080426
835512LV00021B/3453